FASHION PATROL

Written and illustrated by
Kyra Cathcart

My name is Kennedy and there's nothing I hate worse than a bad outfit. I seem to see one every single day!

A
R
T

Like today at lunch, Emma had this ugly smiley-face shirt on. What, are we in the third grade?

And don't get me started on what Aaron was wearing. His big red shoes did not go with his orange hair at all.

And then there was Karley with her love for knee-high sneaker boots and Toni with his oversized pants. And I can't even talk about Brandon!

And Janelle, my best friend Janelle, loved oversized sweatshirts.

I was tired, and I had to do something about it.
So, when I went home, I wrote up some rules to help
everyone.

I'm the fashion patrol, here to protect people from bad outfits and bad choices.

I'm keeping the streets safe from oversized tee-shirts, mixed-matched clothes, and, worst of all, ugly boots.

But it didn't end at school. When I went to the mall and saw Kiki picking out an ugly outfit, I saved her.

Jeans under a skirt! I couldn't let her make that horrible mistake. And poor Katie. Purple was never her color, but she kept wearing it anyway!

They were so ungrateful. They didn't respect fashion rules the way I did. Even my sister, Jayda, and her friends ignored the fashion rules. Yes, I took their things, but it was for their own good!

After a successful week of patrolling, Friday came around.
As soon as I stepped off the bus, I saw something awful.
Everyone had boots on!

So, I did what I do best. I yelled and took anything ugly I could possibly find.

I took sneakers, cowboy boots, summer hats, winter hats, and anything else I could find. Then I saw two of the ugliest outfits of the day. Turns out they were my parents!

One person was wearing a black shirt and yellow pants, and the other had a blue shirt and brown pants on. "Hand 'em over!" I yelled as I looked up.

Jayda told on me, and the other kids did too. The principal told me to give every single bit of clothing back to the kids I took them from.

I guess what I did was wrong. Some people just dress funny, and I couldn't do anything about it.

I guess people have their own style, and that's okay! When people are allowed to express themselves, they come up with some pretty cool ideas.

And if you want to know the truth, different is cool sometimes, even when I don't understand it.